Come Unto Me

10 Comforting Solo Piano Arrangements for Worship

Arranged by Marilynn Ham

Every time I arrange music for solo piano I enjoy the creative process, which is different for each project. This time I let my fingers roam over the keys, discovering new sounds and diverse textures. I also explored ways to musically convey the meaning of each piece's text. As the ideas took shape, I drew inspiration from Matthew 11:28–30:

> Come to me, all you who are weary and burdened, and I will give you rest. Take my yoke upon you and learn from me, for I am gentle and humble in heart, and you will find rest for your souls. For my yoke is easy and my burden is light. (TNIV)

These arrangements are meant to be calming, reflective, restful, and comforting—yet brimming with passion. May this music bring peace to pianists and audiences alike.

ABIDE WITH ME.	2
BREATHE ON ME, BREATH OF GOD	12
COME, THOU FOUNT OF EVERY BLESSING	16
DONA NOBIS PACEM	7
FANTASY ON *LONDONDERRY AIR*	20
HOW LOVELY IS THY DWELLING PLACE	28
I WANT JESUS TO WALK WITH ME	24
JESUS, LOVER OF MY SOUL	33
MORNING HAS BROKEN	38
NEARER, MY GOD, TO THEE, WITH SCHUBERT'S *IMPROMPTU IN G-FLAT MAJOR*, OP. 90, NO. 3	42

Alfred Music Publishing Co., Inc.
P.O. Box 10003
Van Nuys, CA 91410-0003
alfred.com

Copyright © MMXI by Alfred Music Publishing Co., Inc.
All rights reserved. Printed in USA.

No part of this book shall be reproduced, arranged, adapted, recorded, publicly performed, stored in a retrieval system, or transmitted by any means without written permission from the publisher. In order to comply with copyright laws, please apply for such written permission and/or license by contacting the publisher at alfred.com/permissions.

ISBN-10: 0-7390-8389-9
ISBN-13: 978-0-7390-8389-5

Cover Photo
Long Exposure of Stars: © istockphoto / piskunov

(Approx. Performance Time – 4:00)

Abide with Me

William H. Monk
Arr. Marilynn Ham

(Approx. Performance Time – 3:30)

for Jovee Marie

Dona Nobis Pacem
(Grant Us Peace)

Traditional
Arr. Marilynn Ham

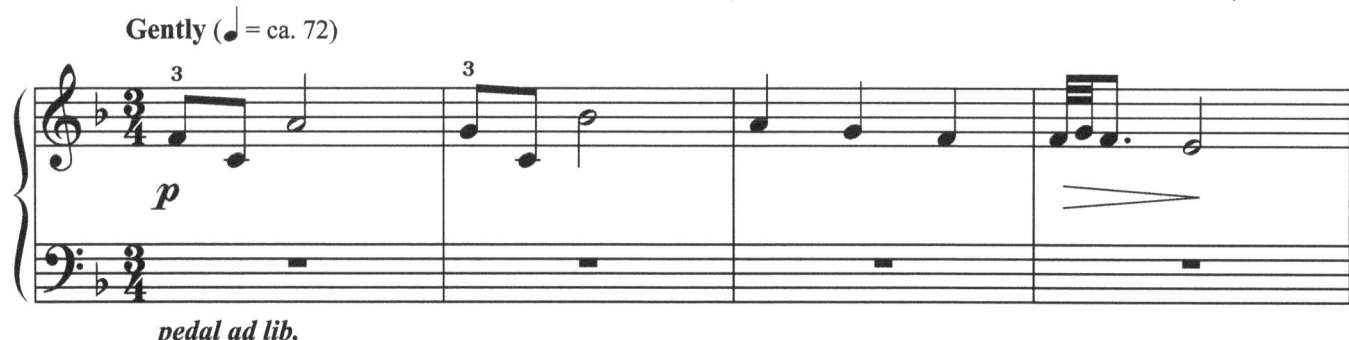
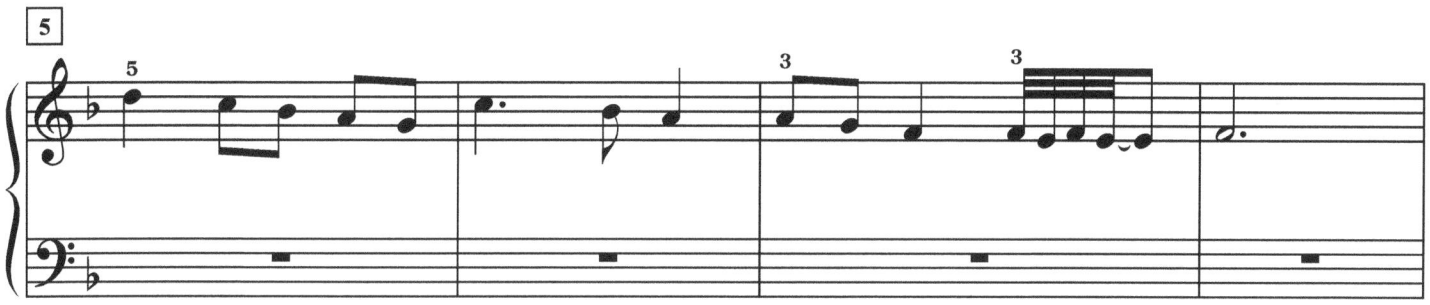
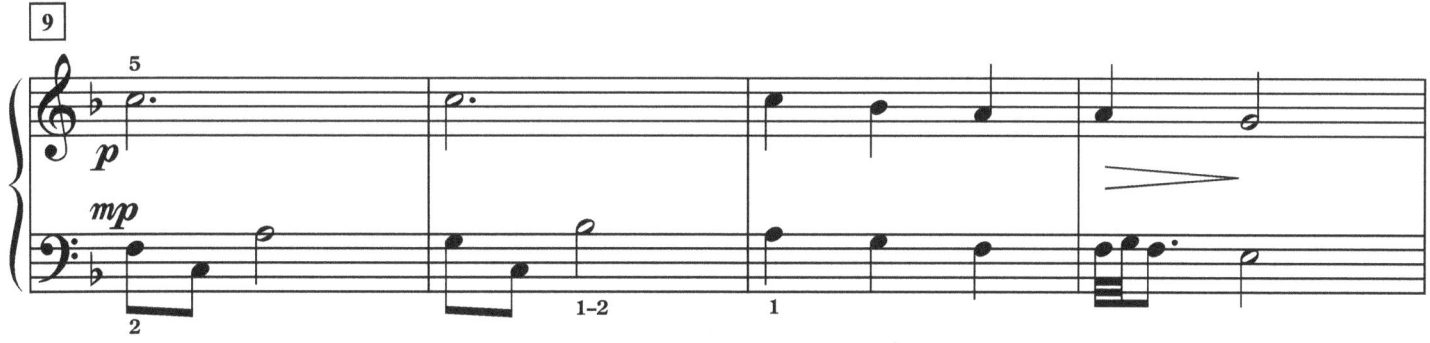

(Approx. Performance Time – 3:15)

Breathe on Me, Breath of God

Robert Jackson
Arr. Marilynn Ham

(Approx. Performance Time – 3:30)

Come, Thou Fount of Every Blessing

Traditional American melody
Arr. Marilynn Ham

(Approx. Performance Time – 4:30)

Fantasy on Londonderry Air

Traditional Irish melody
Arr. Marilynn Ham

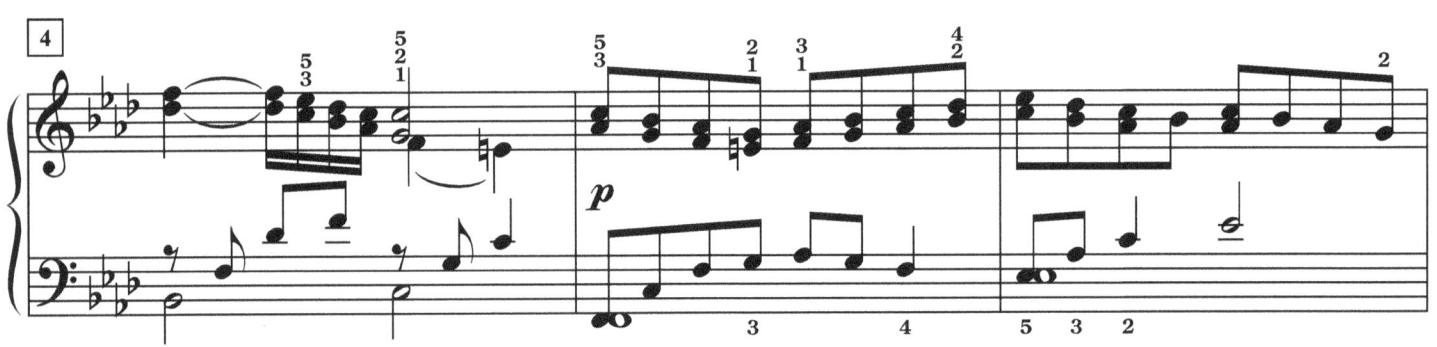

(Approx. Performance Time – 3:15)

I Want Jesus to Walk with Me

Afro-American spiritual
Arr. Marilynn Ham

(Approx. Performance Time – 4:30)

How Lovely Is Thy Dwelling Place

Johannes Brahms
Arr. Marilynn Ham

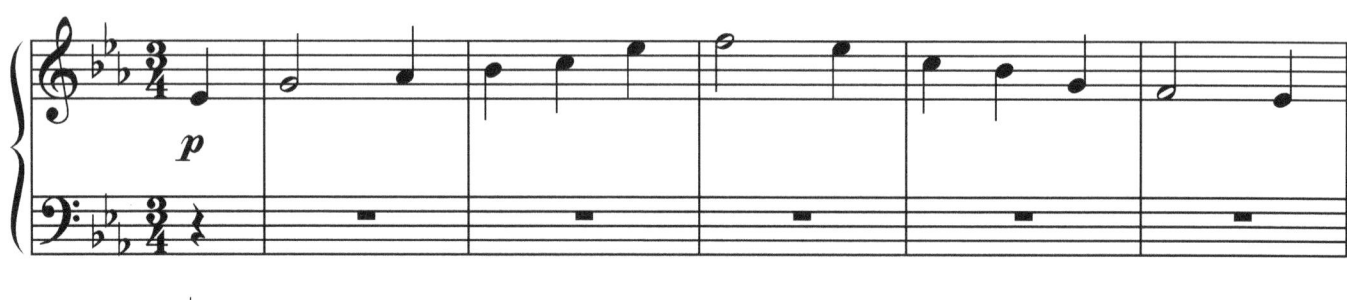

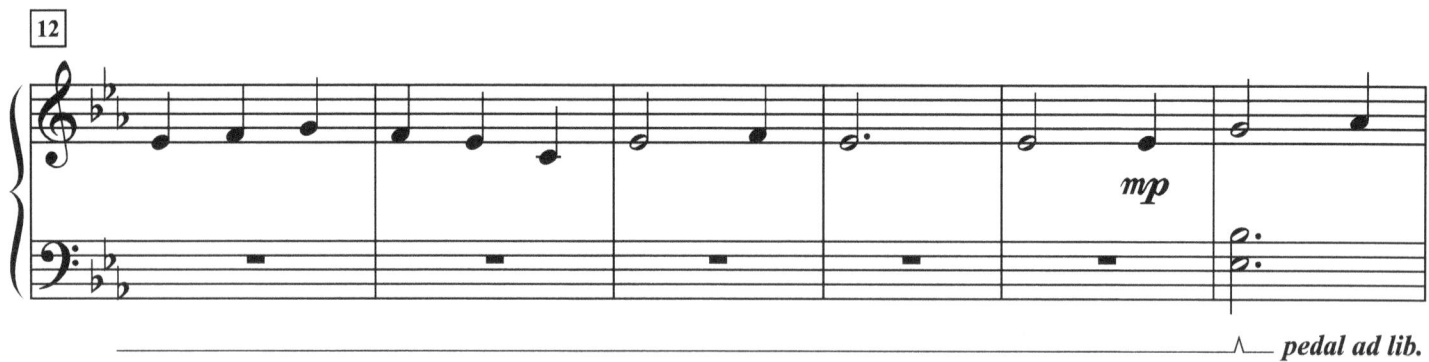

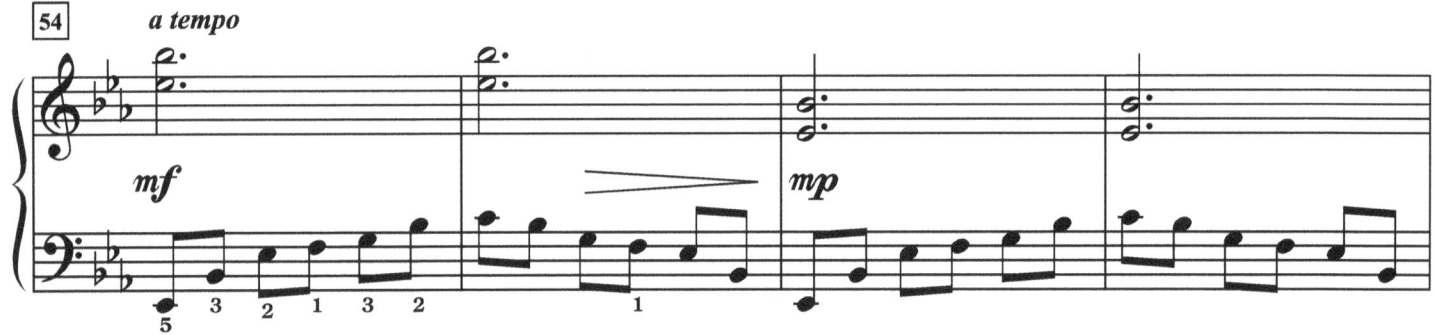

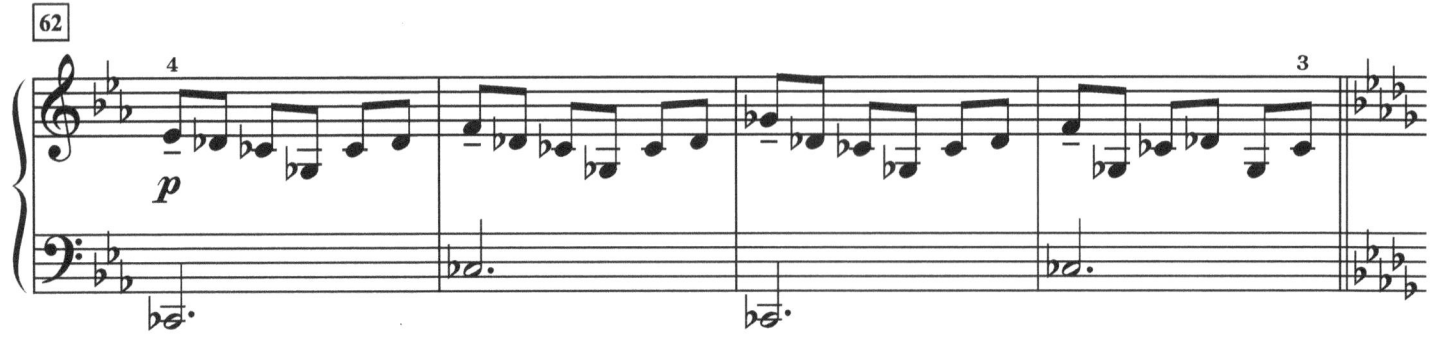

Jesus, Lover of My Soul

Joseph Parry
Arr. Marilynn Ham

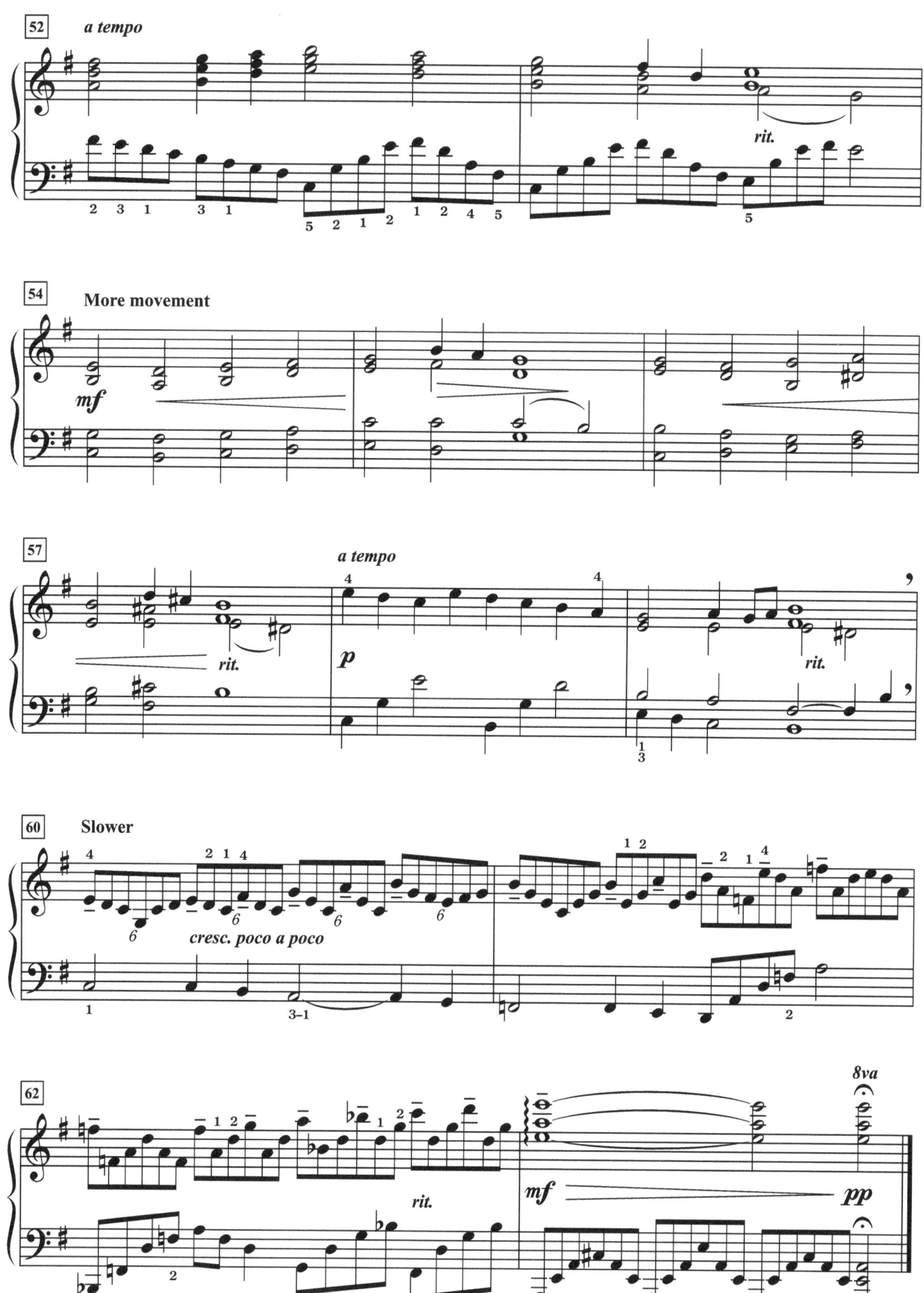

FOR EDEN JOY

Morning Has Broken

Traditional Gaelic melody
Arr. Marilynn Ham

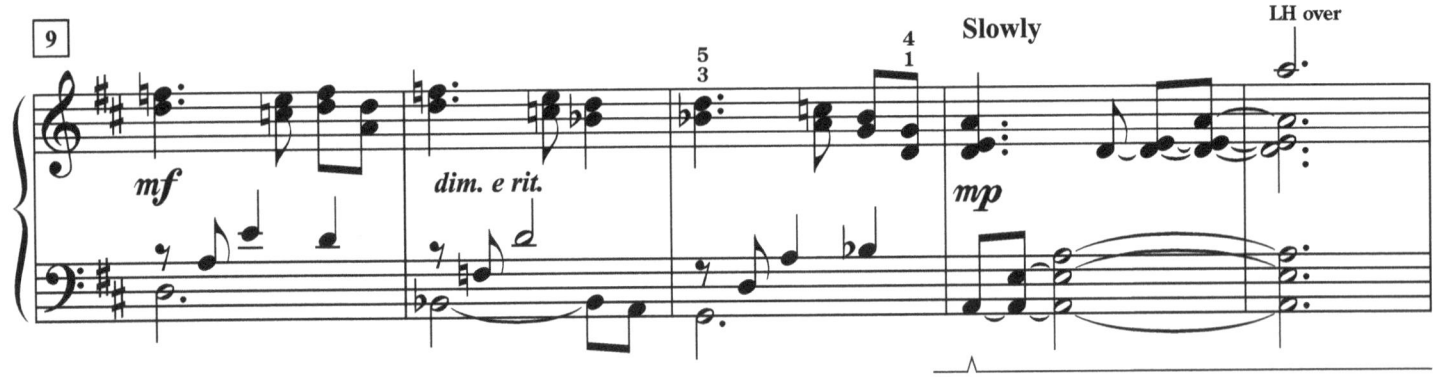

(Approx. Performance Time – 5:45)

Nearer, My God, to Thee
with
Schubert's *Impromptu in G-flat Major*, Op. 90, No. 3

Lowell Mason/Franz Schubert
Arr. Marilynn Ham

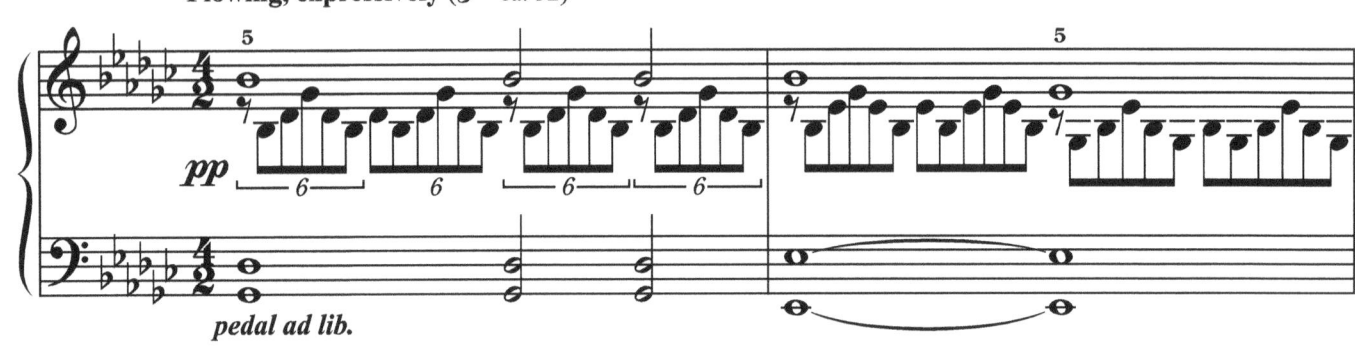

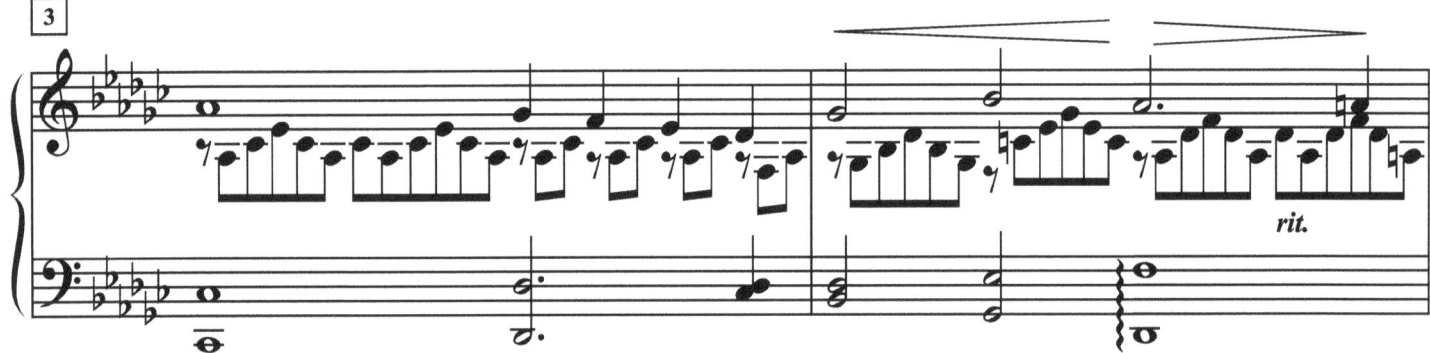

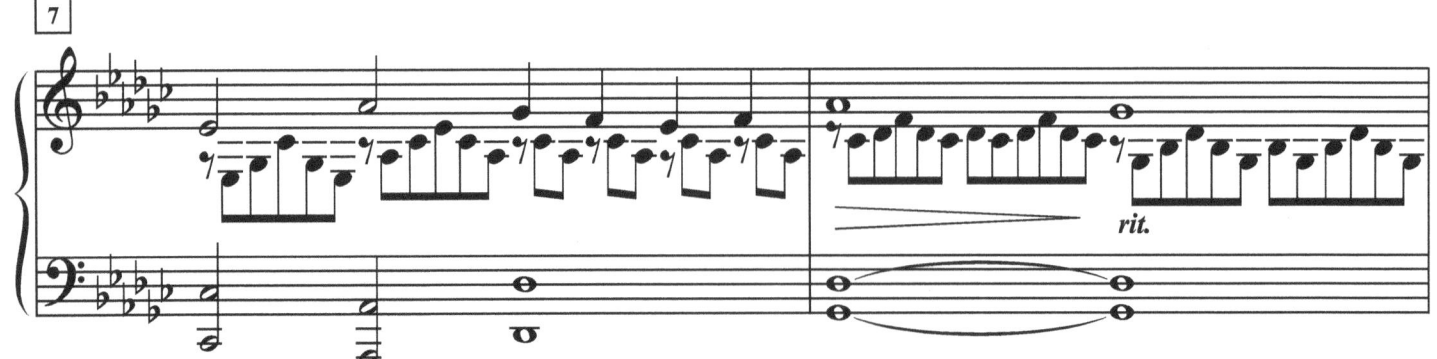

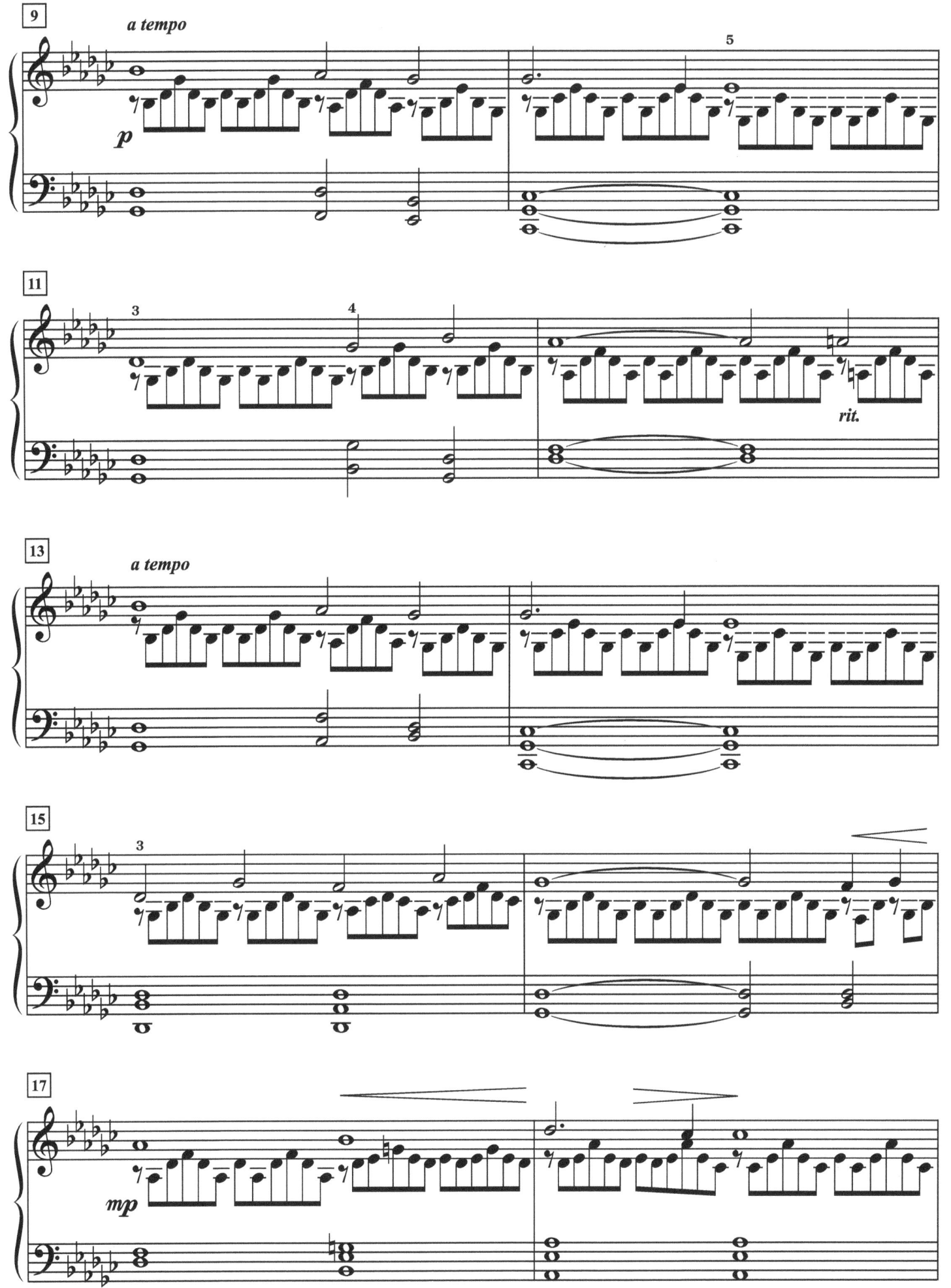

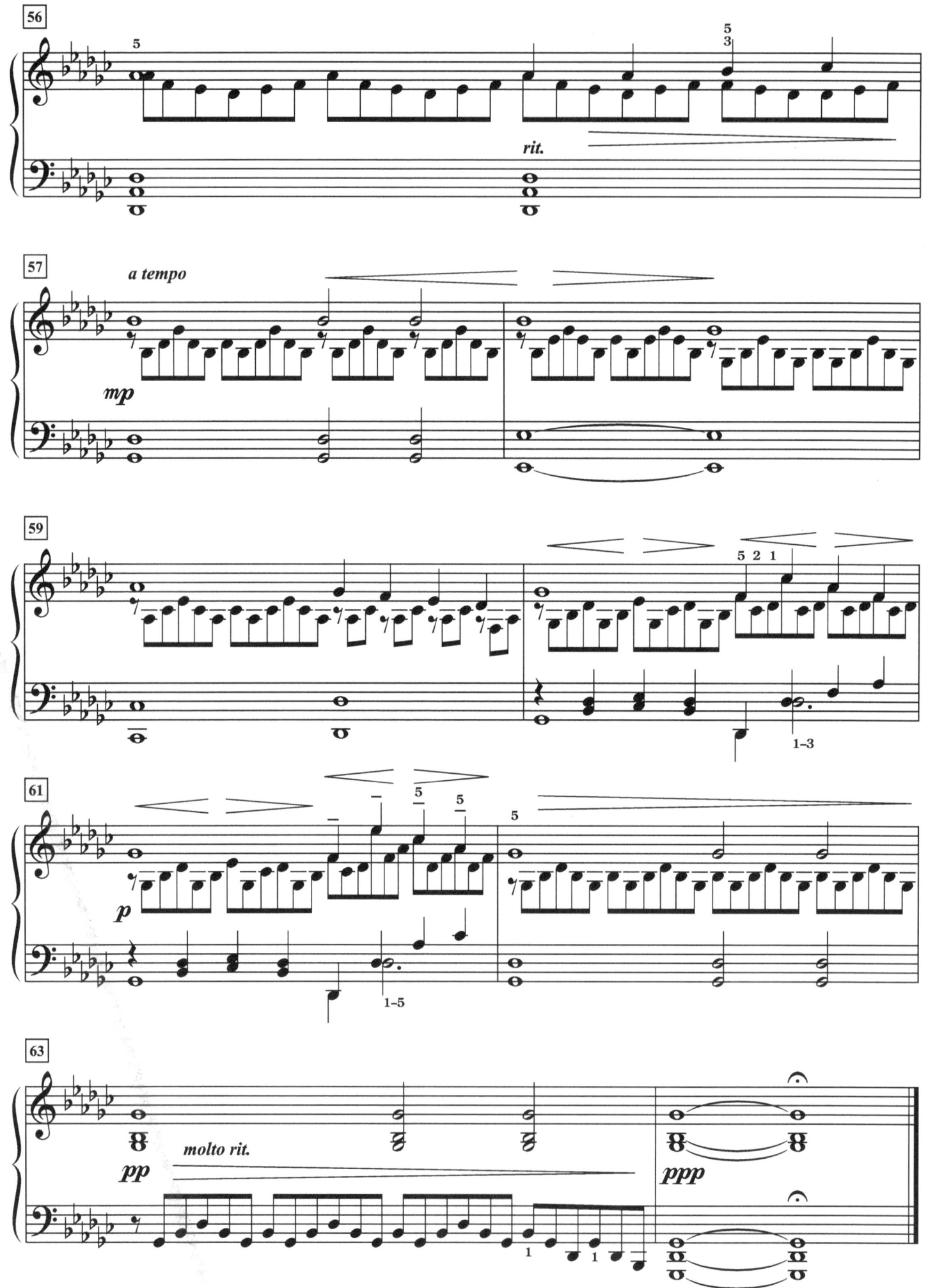